CATS AND LADIES

Cats and Ladies Copyright © *2018* by Melanie Gregs
All rights reserved
Drawings by Melanie Gregs
Cover design by Gerardo Abriola

Melanie Gregs

CATS AND LADIES

"If a fish is the movement of water embodied, given shape, then a cat is a diagram and pattern of subtle air."

Doris Lessing

"The cat is the animal to whom the Creator gave the biggest eye, the softest fur, the most supremely delicate nostrils, a mobile ear, an unrivalled paw and a curved claw borrowed from the rose-tree."

Colette

When God made the world, He chose to put animals in it, and decided to give each whatever it wanted. All the animals formed a long line before His throne, and the cat quietly went to the end of the line. To the elephant and the bear He gave strength, to the rabbit and the deer, swiftness; to the owl, the ability to see at night, to the birds and the butterflies, great beauty; to the fox, cunning; to the monkey, intelligence; to the dog, loyalty; to the lion, courage; to the otter, playfulness. And all these were things the animals begged of God. At last he came to the end of the line, and there sat the little cat, waiting patiently.
"What will YOU have?" God asked the cat.
The cat shrugged modestly. "Oh, whatever scraps you have left over. I don't mind."
"But I'm God. I have everything left over."
"Then I'll have a little of everything, please."
And God gave a great shout of laughter at the cleverness of this small animal, and gave the cat everything she asked for, adding grace and elegance and, only for her, a gentle purr that would always attract humans and assure her a warm and comfortable home.
But he took away her false modesty.

                Lenore Fleischer - The Cat's Pajamas

"I think one reason we admire cats, those of us who do, is their proficience in one-upmanship. They always seem to come out on top, no matter what they are doing, or pretend to do. Rarely do you see a cat discomfited. They have no conscience, and they never regret. Maybe we secretly envy them."

Barbara Webster

"Cats invented self-esteem; there is not an insecure bone in their body."

Erma Bombeck

"What a luxury a cat is, the moments of shocking and startling pleasure in a day, the feel of the beast, the soft sleekness under your palm, the warmth when you wake on a cold night, the grace and charm even in a quite ordinary workaday puss. Cat walks across your room, and in that lonely stalk you see leopard or even panther, or it turns its head to acknowledge you and the yellow blaze of those eyes tells you what an exotic visitor you have here, in this household friend, the cat who purrs as you stroke, or rub his chin, or scratch his head."

    Doris Lessing - The Old Age of El Magnifico

"Cats come and go without ever leaving."

Martha Curtis

Cats sleep anywhere, any table, any chair.
Top of piano, window-ledge, in the middle, on the edge.
Open draw, empty shoe, anybody's lap will do.
Fitted in a cardboard box, in the cupboard with your frocks.
Anywhere! They don't care! Cats sleep anywhere.

    Eleanor Farjeon - Cats Sleep Anywhere

"If there is one spot of sun spilling onto the floor, a cat will find it and soak it up."

Joan Asper McIntosh

"A cat can maintain a position of curled up somnolence on your knee until you are nearly upright. To the last minute she hopes your conscience will get the better of you and you will settle down again."

Pam Brown

"People who love cats have some of the biggest hearts around."

Susan Easterly

"The key to a successful new relationship between a cat and human is patience."

Susan Easterly

*"Of all our sunny world
I wish only for a garden sofa
where a cat is sunning itself.
There I should sit
with a letter at my breast,
a single small letter.
That is what my dream looks like."*

Edith Södergran - A Wish

It rests me to be among beautiful women
why should one always lie about such matters?
I repeat:
It rests me to converse with beautiful women
even though we talk nothing but nonsense,
the purring of the invisible antennae
is both stimulating and delightful.

Ezra Pound - Tame Cat

> *"Woman, poets, and especially artists, like cats; delicate natures only can realize their sensitive nervous systems."*
>
> Helen M. Winslow

He is a beautiful kitty cat
Frank is his name
And around the barnyard
He has risen to fame

Not only does he have
A coat so warm and soft
He's quite the little mouser
Even up in the tall hay loft

He has a certain way
About him, it's a fact
His personality, my friend
Changes how you react

You fall in love so quickly
When Frank comes into the room
For he takes a lot of time
Out of his busy day to groom

He keeps your heart on a string
And this you can take to the bank
When you become a victim of
A charming cat named Frank!

Marilyn Lott - A Cat Named Frank

*"When I'm discouraged, he's empathy incarnate,
purring and rubbing to telegraph his dismay."*

Catheryn Jakobson

*"No matter how tired or wretched I am, a pussycat
sitting in a doorway can divert my mind."*

Mary E. Wilkins Freeman

*"By associating with the cat
one only risks becoming richer."*

Colette

*"I have a luck cat in my arms,
it spins threads of luck.
Luck cat, luck cat,
make for me three things:
make for me a golden ring,
to tell me that I am lucky;
make for me a mirror
to tell me that I am beautiful;
make for me a fan
to waft away my cumbersome thoughts.
Luck cat, luck cat,
spin for me some news of my future!"*

Edith Södergran - Luck Cat

Burly and big, his books among,
Good Samuel Johnson sat,
With frowning brows and wig askew,
His snuff-strewn waistcoat far from new;
So stern and menacing his air,
That neither Black Sam,
nor the maid
To knock or interrupt him dare;
Yet close beside him, unafraid,
Sat Hodge, the cat.
"This participle," the Doctor wrote,
"The modern scholar cavils at,
But," - even as he penned the word,
A soft, protesting note was heard;
The Doctor fumbled with his pen,
The dawning thought took wings and flew,
The sound repeated, come again,
It was a faint, reminding "Mew!"
From Hodge, the cat...
The Dictionary was laid down,
The Doctor tied his vast cravat,
And down the buzzing street he strode,
Taking an often-trodden road,
And halted at a well-known stall:
"Fishmonger," spoke the Doctor gruff,
"Give me six oysters, that is all;
Hodge knows when he has had enough,

Hodge is my cat."
Then home; puss dined and while in sleep
he chased a visionary rat,
His master sat him down again,
Rewrote his page, renibbed his pen;
Each "i" was dotted, each "t" was crossed,
He labored on for all to read,
Nor deemed that time was waste or lost
Spent in supplying the small need
Of Hodge, the cat.
The dear old Doctor! Fierce of mien,
Untidy, arbitrary, fat,
What gentle thought his name enfold!
So generous of his scanty gold.
So quick to love, so hot to scorn,
Kind to all sufferers under heaven,
A tend'rer despot ne'er was born;
His big heart held a corner, even
For Hodge, the cat.

    Sarah Chauncy Woolsey (Susan Coolidge)
                      Hodge the Cat

"Cats look beyond appearances, beyond species entirely, it seems to peer into the heart."

Barbara L. Diamond

"He lives in the halflights in secret places, free and alone, this mysterious little great being whom his mistress calls 'My cat.'"

Margaret Benson

"A cat's behavior is a direct reflection of his feelings."

Carole Wilbourn

"I am indebted to the species of the cat for a particular kind of honorable deceit, for a great control over myself, for characteristic aversion to brutal sounds, and for the need to keep silent for long periods of time."

Colette

"The cat has always been associated with the moon. Like the moon it comes to life at night, escaping from humanity and wandering over housetops with its eyes beaming out through the darkness."

Patricia Dale-Green

"To understand a cat, you must realize that he has has own gifts, his own viewpoint, even his own morality."

Lilian Jackson Braun

"The purr from cat to man says, 'You bring me happiness; I am at peace with you.'"

Barbara L. Diamond

"Cats often devise their own sets of rules that they think we should live by, and they may be quick to chastise us if we fail to adhere to these rules!"

Margaret Reister, D.V.M.

Years saw me still Acasto's mansion grace,
The gentlest, fondest of the tabby race;
Before him frisking through the garden glade,
Or at his feet in quiet slumber laid;
Praised for my glossy back of zebra streak,
And wreaths of jet encircling round my neck;
Soft paws that ne'er extend the clawing nail,
The snowy whisker and the sinuous tail;
Now feeble age each glazing eyeball dims,
And pain has stiffened these once supple limbs;
Fate of eight lives the forfeit gasp obtains,
And e'en the ninth creeps languid through my veins.
Much sure of good the future has in store,
When on my master's hearth I bask no more,
In those blest climes, where fishes oft forsake
The winding river and the glassy lake;
There, as our silent-footed race behold
The crimson spots and fins of lucid gold,
Venturing without the shielding waves to play,
They gasp on shelving banks, our easy prey:
While birds unwinged hop careless o'er the ground,
And the plump mouse incessant trots around,
Near wells of cream that mortals never skim,
Warm marum creeping round their shallow brim;
Where green valerian tufts, luxuriant spread,

Cleanse the sleek hide and form the fragrant bed.
Yet, stern dispenser of the final blow,
Before thou lay'st an aged grimalkin low,
Bend to her last request a gracious ear,
Some days, some few short days, to linger here;
So to the guardian of his tabby's weal
Shall softest purrs these tender truths reveal:
'Ne'er shall thy now expiring puss forget
To thy kind care her long-enduring debt,
Nor shall the joys that painless realms decree
Efface the comforts once bestowed by thee;
To countless mice thy chicken-bones preferred,
Thy toast to golden fish and wingless bird;
O'er marum borders and valerian bed
Thy Selima shall bend her moping head,
Sigh that no more she climbs, with grateful glee,
Thy downy sofa and thy cradling knee;
Nay, e'en at founts of cream shall sullen swear,
Since thou, her more loved master, art not there.'

Anna Seward - An Old Cat's Dying Soliloquy

"I will always remember the olive-eyed tabby who taught me that not all relationships are meant to last a lifetime. Sometimes just an hour is enough to touch your heart."

Barbara L. Diamond

"If there were to be a universal sound depicting peace, I would surely vote for the purr."

Barbara L. Diamond

"The constant challenge to decipher feline behavior is perhaps one of the most fascinating qualities of owning a cat."

Carole Wilbourn

"A cat can purr its way out of anything."

Donna McCrohan

*There was once a cat called
Trouble-some Mac'fee,
who had a bad habit,
of inviting himself to tea.
When the clock struck four,
he would tap on the door,
meow and scrach,
then lift up the latch.
He never had a thought,
for dear Aunt Mable,
because he would rush right in,
and jump straight on the table.
He would steal a cake,
from of the plate,
then run back through the door,
and out of the gate.*

Mac-fee Mac-fee,
always there for tea.
Now Mac-fee played a game
called, hide n seek.
At one time he went missing,
for over a week.
Aunt Mable said
'has he gone for good,
but was there any reason
why he should!
No one saw him,
hair or hide,
We serched all over,
far and wide.
Then on a Friday, just before tea
who should turn up,
our trouble-some Mac-Fee
His paws were dirty,
and his coat was shabby,
but oh how we loved,
that dear old tabby.
Mac-Fee Mac-Fee,
always there for tea.
Aunt Mable had passed on,
and so had her cake,
and poor Mac-Fee,
was getting thin as rake.

When the clock struck four,
he went next door,
to see what tit bits,
he could score.
Alas the cake was not the same,
so old Mac-Fee,
came home again.
Poor Mac-Fee he missed aunt Mable,
and all the cakes,
that were laid on the table.
Nine lives were leaving, poor Mac-Fee,
and his troublesome days were over,
and now his buried in a field,
under a bed of clover.

Sylvia Spencer - The Cat That Came To Tea

"It (the Cheshire Cat) vanished quite slowly, beiginning with the end of the tail, and ending with the grin, which remained some time after the rest of it had gone."

Colette

"A kitten is the most irresistible comedian in the world. Its wide-open eyes gleam with wonder and mirth. It darts madly at nothing at all, and then, as though suddenly checked in the pursuit, prances sideways on its hind legs with ridiculous agility and zeal."

Agnes Repplier

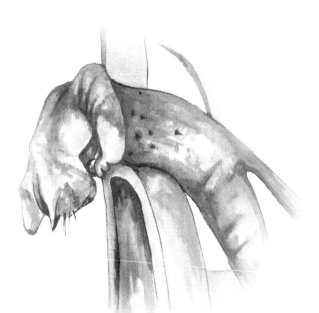

*"Because his long, white whiskers tickled,
I began every day laughing."*

Janet F. Faure

*"The playful kitten with its pretty little tigerish gambole
is infinitely more amusing than half the people
one is obliged to live with in the world."*

Lady Sydney Morgan

"Perhaps a child, like a cat, is so much inside of himself that he does not see himself in the mirror."

Anais Nin - The Diary of Anais Nin, Vol II

"Cats can work out mathematically the exact place to sit that will cause most inconvenience."

Pam Brown

"A kitten is chiefly remarkable for rushing about like mad at nothing whatever, and generally stopping before it gets there."

Agnes Repplier

"Any cat who misses a mouse pretends it was aiming for the dead leaf."

Charlotte Gray

He's nothing much but fur
And two round eyes of blue,
He has a giant purr
And a midget mew.
He darts and pats the air,
He starts and cocks his ear,
When there is nothing there
For him to see and hear.
He runs around in rings,
But why we cannot tell;
With sideways leaps he springs
At things invisible -
Then half-way through a leap
His startled eyeballs close,
And he drops off to sleep
With one paw on his nose.

                        Eleanor Farjeon - A Kitten

My cat is entertaining
As he bolts and rolls
I smile and shake my head
My laughter I am not restraining

Lying on his back
And pawing the air
As though rolling an invisible ball
Now he's racing as though on the attack

Leaping to the couch and soaring
To the rug with a half twist
Landing on all four paws…
I'd rate that a ten if I were scoring

Theresa Ann Moore - My Cat The Acrobat

"There is nothing in the animal world, to my mind, more delightful than grown cats at play. They are so swift and light and graceful, so subtle and designing, and yet so richly comical."

Monica Edwards

"Places to look: behind the books in the bookshelf, any cupboard with a gap too small for any cat to squeeze through, the top of anything sheer, under anything too low for a cat to squash under and inside the piano."

Roseanne Ambrose-Brown

There was A Cat left in a house
Whose occupants long gone
He comes and goes
With spotted nose
To wander there alone
Through vacant rooms
He hops and zooms
No ball of thread has he
Past moldy walls
Down doorless halls
He plays with hearty glee
Up cobwebbed chairs
Down rusty stairs
No whiney tigers gloom
He darts about
With fearless snout
In dark, in dust and doom

Louise Bizzari - A Cat

"After scolding one's cat one looks into its face and is seized by the ugly suspicion that it understood every word. And has filed it for reference."

Charlotte Gray

"Who needs television when you have cats?"

Lori Spigelmyer

"If your cat falls out of a tree, go indoors to laugh."

Patricia Hitchcock

"The trouble with sharing one's bed with cats is that they'd rather sleep on you than beside you."

Pam Brown

"A cat allows you to sleep on the bed. On the edge."

Jenny de Vries

"Any household with at least one feline member has no need for an alarm clock."

Louise A. Belcher

*"I found out why cats drink out of the toilet.
My mother told me it's because the water is cold in there.
And I'm like: How did my mother know that?"*

Wendy Liebman

A black cat crossed my path
On a night of a full moon
He was carrying a pack on his back
And dancing around like a loon.

I thought it was a funny sight
I couldn't believe my eyes
Then I saw a ghostly cat
In a transparent disguise.

His eyes glowed like fire
In the darkened night
My hands grew cold
I was filled with fright.

Just then the ghostly cat
Found the black cat by a tree
They both did a jig
And started singing merrily.

I was no longer scared
As they danced 'round and 'round
It was an unusual scene
And an unusual sound.

They sang Halloween songs
About pumpkins and goblins and bats
And as they sang
Along came about fifty other cats.

They all joined in
The sound grew so loud
But it was a happy sound
From a jolly crowd.

All of the cats were dancing
And having a good time
Then the ghostly cat invited me
To have a bite of a lime.

I told him it would be sour
He said "Well, come dance instead"
So I joined the singing cats
And danced with a cat named Fred.

He moved around quite fast
Hopping left and right
We both danced and danced
Deep into the night.

At last I had enough
I couldn't dance anymore
So I said good-bye to all the cats
And Fred walked me to my door.

He asked if he could come in
I said "my two cats would probably mind"
So he said "I'll see you around"
I said "I had a nice time."

One year went by
Halloween was here again
A black cat crossed my path
I knew the party was about to begin.

Happy Halloween.

Connie Webb - A Black Cat Crossed My Path

"When adressed, a gentleman cat does not move a muscle. He looks as if he hasn't heard."

Mary Sarton

I put down my book, The Meaning of Zen,
and see the cat smiling into her fur as she
delicately combs it with her rough pink tongue.
"Cat, I would lend you this book to study
but it appears you have already read it."
She looks up and gives me her full gaze.
"Don't be ridiculous" she purrs, "I wrote it."

                    Dilys Laing - from "Miao"

Cat!
Atter her, atter her,
Sleeky flatterer,
Spitfire chatterer,
Scatter her, scatter her
Wuff!
Wuff!
Treat her rough!
Git her, git her,
Whiskery spitter!
Catch her, catch her,
Green-eyed scratcher!
Slathery
Slithery
Hisser,
Don't miss her!
Run till you're dithery,
Hithery
Thithery
Pfitts! pfitts!
How she spits!
Spitch! Spatch!
Can't she scratch!
Scritching the bark
Of the sycamore-tree,
She's reached her ark
And's hissing at me

Pfitts!Pfitts!
Wuff! Wuff!
Scat,
Cat!
That's
That!

Eleanor Farjeon - *Cat!*

"I never married because there was no need. I have three pets at home which answer the same purpose as a husband. I have a dog which growls every morning, a parrot which swears all afternoon, and a cat that comes home late at night."

Maria Corelli

"I write so much because my cat sits on my lap. She purrs so I don't want to get up. She's so much more calming than my husband."

Joyce Carol Oates

"Recently we were discussing the possibility of making one of our cats Pope, and we decided that the fact that she was not Italian, and was female, made the third point, that she was a cat, irrelevant."

Katharine Whitehorn Leicester

"A catless writer is almost inconceivable. It's a perverse taste, really, since it would be easier to write with a herd of buffalo in the room than even one cat; they make nests in the notes and bite the end of the pen and walk on the typewriter keys."

Barbara H

"Most of us rather like our cats to have a streak of wickedness. I should not feel quite easy in the company of any cat that walked about the house with a saintly expression"

Beverly Nichols

"Dogs come when they're called; cats take a message and get back to you later."

Mary Bly

"If a homeless cat could talk, it would probably say, 'Give me shelter, food, companionship and love, and I will be yours for life!"

Susan Easterly

"I saw the most beautiful cat today. It was sitting by the side of the road, its two front feet neatly and graciously together. Then it gravely swished around its tail to completely encircle itself. It was so fit and beautifully neat, that gesture, and so self-satisfied, so complacent."

Ann Morrow Lindbergher

A tiny tabby kitten, with sad brown eyes.
Sat on the porch of a broken down house.
He was about to become homeless,
without any food, not even a mouse.

I stood and gazed at this poor lonely cat.
Shook my head and placed him in my hat.
A long drive across the city we drove.
Now Tiger sits cozily in front of our stove.

    Melvina Germain - Our Cat (Tiger)

One day you wandered into my view.
Your fur was tufted and ridiculously askew.
You were a confused vagabond without a home.
It was my intention that you would continue to roam.

You looked at me like we had known each other before.
As though to say, 'Recognize me, feed me... open the door.'
Your delving green eyes pried open my heart with a plea.
Your clawless paws managed to magnetically attach to me.

Your persuasive ways and purring motor have earned you a ticket.
This is your home and you're an important part of our family unit.
You now fill a previously nonexistent void with constant affection.
Stray cat of mine, you no longer have to worry about rejection.

                        Theresa Ann Moore - Stray Cat

"I regard cats as one of the great joys in the world. I see them as a gift of highest order."

Trisha McCagh

"How nice it is to think that feline dreams, like our own, are painted with creative brush strokes from time to time. Perhaps my cats and I even share the same dream: a world where all kittens are wanted and loved, and where every cat has a safe, warm place to sleep... and to dream."

Barbara L. Diamond

"When your cat rubs the side of its face along your leg, it's affectionately marking you with its scent, identifying you as its private property, saying, in effect, 'You belong to me'."

                                Susan McDonough, D.M.V.

"When you're special to a cat, you're special indeed... she brings to you the gift of her preference of you, the sight of you, the sound of your voice, the touch of your hand."

                                        Leonore Fleisher

"Her function is to sit and be admired."

Georgina Strickland Gates

"The cat is above all things, a dramatist."

Margaret Benson

*"Cats like doors left open
in case they change their minds."*

Rosemary Nisbet

"At dinner time he would sit in a corner, concentrating, and suddenly they would say, 'Time to feed the cat,' as if it were their own idea."

Lilian Jackson Braun

The cat is free;
No tether he
Will wear in circumspect.

Ah but the eyes
And jealous cries
We hold in dire respect.

Disdains the call,
A prison wall
Will never him attract.

Yet he betrays
His freedom's ways
For one kind word and pat.

                      Adeline Foster - The Cat Is Free

"It always gives me a shiver when I see a cat seeing what I can't see."

Eleanor Farjeon

"Sleeping together is a euphemism for people, but tantamount to marriage with cats."

Marge Percy

"The way to get on with a cat is to treat it as an equal or even better, as the superior it knows itself to be."

Elizabeth Peters

"Cats are dogs with a college education"

Grace Hodgson

"Purring would seem to be, in her case, an automatic safety valve device for dealing with happiness overflow."

Monica Edwards

"A cat sees no good reason why it should obey another animal, even if it does stand on two legs."

Sarah Thompson

"People that hate cats will come back as mice in their next life."

Faith Resnick

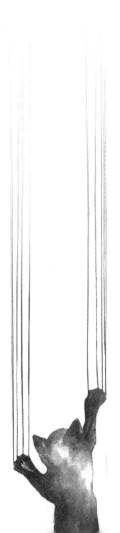

Made in United States
Orlando, FL
20 December 2024